The Ballad of Emperor Norton

The Ballad of Emperor Norton

Garrett Buhl Robinson

Poet in the Park
In Humanity I see Grace, Beauty and Dignity.

Parts of this book have been published in earlier collections.

The prologue was previous published as "Emperor Norton's Test of Will" from the collection *Broken Open*.

"Emperor Norton Saves San Francisco" was previous published as "Emperor Norton in Love" in *Always Here Always Odd*.

"Emperor Norton vs. the Diabolic Machine" was published as a chapbook in 2020.

Poet in the Park and the *Solemn Swan* colophon are trademarks registered with the United States Patent and Trademark Offices

Special thanks to RB, JP and MD.

Garrett Buhl Robinson © 2021
All Rights Reserved

Poet in the Park®
In Humanity I see Grace, Beauty and Dignity.

PoetinthePark.com

Table of Content

Prologue
Emperor Norton's Command _____ 1

Part I
Emperor Norton Saves San Francisco

The Long Arms of Emperor Norton _____ 9
Emperor Norton Saves San Francisco _____ 13
Emperor Norton's Theory of Gravity _____ 18

Part II
Emperor Norton vs. the Diabolic Machine

Norton Invents the Washing Machine _____ 25
Parading with the Parrots _____ 28
Taking a Stand against Exploitation _____ 29
Rallying his Troops _____ 40
The Siege of the Fortress of Oppression ____ 44
The Fearsome Battle _____ 49

Part III
The Trial of Emperor Norton

Emperor Norton Plays the Market _____ 67
Emperor Norton in Court _____ 72

Epilogue
Emperor Norton's Everlasting Day _____ 95

For beautiful San Francisco

&

for my friend
Ranger Bob of New York City

who asked me to write a poem about
Emperor Norton

— Well, here it is!

Prologue —
Emperor Norton's Command

Being Emperor Norton
    is not an easy task,
when every day his regal reign
    is filled with countless tests.

As he parades before the taverns
    that pour out merriment
the crowds beg him to come inside
    for his accompaniment.

They offer him a chair to sit
    right at the table's head,
and then they gather at his side
    to hear all that he says.

They fill a handsome mug with beer
    and serve it to their friend,
and stand around so they can hear
    the stories that he wends.

Then jostling through the happy place
    a man shoves through the crowd,
and stands before the Emperor,
    a seething, spiteful lout.

Prologue

Then as the crowd all stand in awe
    the man shrieks his complaint:
"I know they call you Emperor,
    in some obnoxious game,

but I must claim the contrary,
    despite what I have heard,
to call Falstaff an Emperor
    is silly and absurd."

The Noble Emp'ror Norton
    turns toward the stranger's face,
to see if these insulting words
    are simply made in play.

The stranger then cannot resist
    to add more snorting brays,
dismissing doubts whether the ass
    has any more to say.

"How can you waste all of your time
    just swilling quaffs of beer,
as if you do not have a care
    how you'll walk out of here?

"Who would appoint you Emperor
    on which you stake your fame,
upon what powers do you rule,
    how can you make this claim?"

The Ballad of Emperor Norton

The Emp'ror Norton sat at ease
    to hear this stranger's say
and let him vent out angrily
    of what upset his day.

Then gently parting his mustache
    and stroking his soft beard,
he slowly lifts his frothy mug
    to tipple some cold beer.

He swells his chest with a deep breath,
    releases a sweet sigh,
then tranquilly explains before
    the man stirs up a fight.

"My title and authority
    is known across the land
and is confirmed as everyone
    obeys my one command."

Perhaps the answer is too clear,
    perhaps he thinks it curt,
because the man quickly recoils
    as if these words had hurt.

Then clenching fists at either side,
    his face boils red with heat
then he begins to holler out
    while stamping with his feet.

Prologue

"How can you utter such a thing?
  How can you make that claim?
I know some call you Emperor,
  but I say you're insane.

"The ministers and Presidents,
  the judges who preside,
they all work hard to lead us on
  and keep us in the right.

"Yet still the people never fail
  to stray all of the time.
No leader's ever had the strength
  to keep us all in line."

Then Norton calmly shakes his head,
  astonished with his guest,
then bellows out with hearty laughs
  that bounce his epaulets.

Then with the breadth of a short pause
  sealed in a herring can
the Emp'ror speaks to make it plain
  so all could understand.

"My friend your anger is in vain,
  your fury's for yourself,
and with my magnanimity
  I'll offer you some help.

The Ballad of Emperor Norton

"It's true that I have made the claim
    as Emp'ror in my time,
my irresistible command
    can never be denied.

"Friend, let your heart by merry,
    come and drink your fill,
the one command that I have made
    is that we do just as we will."

Part I
Emperor Norton
Saves
San Francisco

The long arms of Emperor Norton embrace everything!

On yet another sunny day
    on Broadway at North Beach
the Royal Emp'ror Norton
    can once again be seen.

And on this day as every day
    a crowd has gathered round
as if they have been magnetized
    by melodies of sound.

But more than just his tone of voice
    there is a charming sight,
the same as the enchanting way
    that life is drawn to light.

The people's cheeks will blush rose red,
    their faces shine with smiles
and sometimes you can almost see
    the sun rise in their eyes.

But then there is a scuffling huff
    as shoves disturb the crowd
while someone pushes his way through
    with scowls of his dour frown.

Emperor Norton Embraces Everything

The man proclaims an urgent task
    to which he must attend
but all he ever seems to do
    is insult and offend.

Each person has direction,
    a voice for their own say,
but all this guy has ever said
    is: "You're all in my way!"

It's like he has a special call
    for others to feel worse
and this begrudging task in life
    is his resolved purpose.

But the reigning Emp'ror Norton
    cannot be pushed aside,
the solid place of his stature
    is firm where he resides.

And complicating even more
    this man's repellency,
is Norton tends to embrace all
    who are within his reach.

So even in his grumbles,
    the man may squirm and tug
but finds himself warmly locked up
    in Norton's royal hug.

The Ballad of Emperor Norton

Released from Norton's warm embrace
    he's lighter on his feet
and all the bitter spite of life
    has suddenly turned sweet.

He staggers back in his surprise
    tongue tied for what to say
at how that gesture of acceptance
    brightened his glum day.

And suddenly astonishment
    about the quickened change
has turned his life so that he sees
    the world in a new way.

Then fumbling for some awkward words
    to fit into a phrase
he asks how Emp'ror Norton
    had cured him of his rage.

His day was ruined from the start
    before he left his bed.
As soon as he opened his eyes
    he felt a dismal dread.

We all have obligations
    along obstructed paths
and all his snarling obstacles
    would never let him pass.

Emperor Norton Embraces Everything

The sunny fields beyond the hills
    that he had sought to find
were always blighted with the night
    the time that he arrived.

He found the gentle Emperor
    was standing in his way
but somehow Norton had transformed
    cold night into warm day.

Is this event a miracle?
    There's some who'd make that claim.
Yet Emperor Norton calmly says
    it's easy to explain:

"Don't feel you must deal like with like,
    a measure for a measure,
the way to truly conquer hate
    is with a friendly gesture."

Emperor Norton applies the Theory of Love to save San Francisco

But then the crowd was quite perplexed
    at Norton's noble stand
and how he mustered up the spunk
    to face the troubled land.

Incredulous a man protests
    if love can conquer hate
and doubtful that it can be done
    he has these words to say.

"Our lives are very complicated
    and answers are not clear,
it is a foolish strategy
    to laugh off hate and fear.

"There are the raging fires of war,
    aggressive, angry powers,
one cannot hope to make the peace
    by waving round a flower.

"And even if a person could,
    the act would still disrupt,
that poor, defenseless, helpless plant
    still had its flower plucked.

Emperor Norton Saves San Francisco

"How did the flower make offense?
    Whatever is the reason?
To make the knives turned on the plant
    and hack it into pieces?

"Our history has always shown
    what's innocent and nice
is always first to be led to
    the bloody sacrifice."

Then Emp'ror Norton calms the crowd
    with nothing but a sigh,
then with the twinkle in his eye
    presents his tickled smile.

The crowd moves closer so to hear
    how Norton will reply
and listens tight with all their might
    expecting something wry.

Then after a suspenseful pause
    the picture is reframed
as Norton soothes the patient crowd
    and tranquilly explains:

"The quibbling can go on forever
    to parse infinity,
but yet the truth often eludes
    our rationality.

The Ballad of Emperor Norton

"I'm one who does admire the plants,
    the flowers and the fruits,
the branching tips of tender stems,
    the deepening of roots.

"The flowers bloom so to allure
    with fragrant nectars sweet,
and I believe they're best admired
    with plants still in one piece.

"We cannot claim we love something
    then clip it for our use.
The life must stay complete and whole
    to thrive and to produce.

"Of course this is beside the point,
    please don't let me digress
but often the tangential thoughts
    enlighten and impress.

"Besides this little floral flourish,
    the question that you asked
is can a peaceful disposition
    divert a fierce attack?

"And keep in mind that this is not
    a futile abstract tactic.
This theory has been smartly proved.
    I've put it into practice.

Emperor Norton Saves San Francisco

"One night there was an angry mob
    that marched throughout the city,
they were determined to destroy
    without a drop of pity.

"They were all irked and riled about
    our life's humiliations
and they all sought to dissipate
    their furious frustrations.

"Too often when we're aggravated
    our anger turns to shame
because we often turn our rage
    on those who aren't to blame.

"This mob with torches in their hands
    were crazed to burn things down
and stormed the city streets that night
    inciting the whole town.

"I faced the mob right in the street,
    before the flickering flames,
I knew none of them were themselves
    but crazy with their rage.

"Then where I stood they stopped their march
    with stunned, bewildered stares
and then I started to recite
    the lines of the Lord's Prayer.

The Ballad of Emperor Norton

"I knew I was against the worst,
    it had to get much better
and then I reached the final line
    concluding with forever.

"When I recited the whole prayer
    up to the very end,
I then returned to the first line
    to say it once again.

"Again, again I said the prayer
    to hot and angry faces,
and slowly watched the fearsome heat
    cool into sweetened graces.

"Then slowly all the raucous noise
    was peaceful in no time,
so calm we thought that we could hear
    stars twinkling in the sky.

"The flames still burned, but differently,
    a change in wind was blown,
the flames would not burn down the town,
    their light now led them home."

Emperor Norton's Theory of Gravity

But then another rousing voice
>has yet another question
as if the crowd ceaselessly craves
>Norton's explanations.

"Your story's sweet and wonderful
>except for just one word —
How could the Royal Emperor
>be subject to a Lord?"

The Emperor took pause again
>and arches up his brow.
Not curious at what they asked
>but puzzled by their doubt.

Then with a single sip of wine
>to tune his vocal chords
he opens up the sluice again
>for his profuse discourse —

"We all have guides to all our lives
>of this you can believe
and I am subject to these rules
>since I had been conceived.

The Ballad of Emperor Norton

"Those rules align our different lives
    so we may interact,
then we can compensate each other
    for what we each may lack.

"The shops of bakers have the bread,
    the butchers have the meat.
The vaulted banks secure the cash
    and trolleys rest our feet.

"But when regarding our positions
    refrain from hasty judgement,
those who are held to be up high
    have others up above them.

"And as the ruling Emperor,
    there's something you must see,
I'm really not up on the top
    but under everything.

"And all my grandeur and my grace
    and willingness to please
is for my station's dedication
    to the *noblesse oblige*.

"I march around like a parade
    in step with my own time
but underneath my plum panache
    you'll find my humble mind.

Emperor Norton's Theory of Gravity

"I'm working all the day and night
    performing dutifully,
there is no way I will neglect
    responsibilities.

"And if I strayed for just a wink
    so my attention lapsed,
there is a terrible concern
    the world might then collapse."

Then with this claim there is a stir,
    that grumbles with discord,
and one voice speaks above the rest
    to ask for a report.

"Please tell us Emp'ror Norton,
    we'd love to hear you say
exactly what this service is
    that saves us every day.

"Each day we see you in the streets,
    each night you're in the bar,
what is this duty you perform
    that lights our guiding star?"

Perhaps the question was too easy
    and served up on a platter
but Norton gobbled it right up
    with dollops of his laughter.

The Ballad of Emperor Norton

"Have not you seen day after day
    and spanning the whole year
how tirelessly I work away
    to keep all in good cheer?

"I know some try to criticize
    and call it frivolous,
this isn't idle jollity
    or wasteful silliness.

"Every city has a hospital,
    and this I know is true
that getting people to feel better
    is what they're made to do.

"Our health is how we feel,
    I'm not just having fun,
the service I provide is real
    and helps out everyone.

"My prescription is for merriment,
    is that not understood?
I'm helping us to not feel bad
    by making us feel good.

"And if you ask who is my Lord
    it's not one up above,
it is something that's in us all —
    our Everlasting Love.

Emperor Norton's Theory of Gravity

"Love is the most tenacious force
    for all society
and just as universal
    as Newton's gravity.

"Some people say it's of the mind,
    and others of the heart,
without it though there is no doubt
    we'd quickly fall apart.

"It can compel us while it binds us
    and guides us through our lives.
It is a vital quality
    to help us to survive.

"Sometimes it comes quite easily,
    you hardly have to try,
like when you brighten someone's day
    with a friendly smile."

Then Emp'ror Norton turns around
    and whiskers on his way,
fulfilling all his errant quests
    with his good deed today.

Some say he's Don Quixote,
    the Falstaff for his day,
but Royal Emp'ror Norton
    is unique in every way.

Part II

Emperor Norton vs. the Diabolic Machine

Emperor Norton invents the Washing Machine after Breakfast

Reliably every morning
    or at least by afternoon,
the Royal Emp'ror Norton
    arises from his snooze.

He brews a cup of steaming tea
    that's strong and stoutly steeped
although sometimes the tea is brewed
    from eucalyptus leaves.

Perhaps it's from necessity
    or of his own invention
as Emp'ror Norton certainly
    diverges from convention.

And when he's flush with fortune
    and rises from his bed
he will prepare an omelette
    of hardy ostrich eggs.

Then when he's done with breakfast
    he fills the tub to clean,
he's nobly obligated
    to keep the best hygiene.

Norton Invents the Washing Machine

And here again he demonstrates
    his ingenuity
and how resourceful he can be
    to live efficiently.

Now Norton's famous uniform
    is vital to his life.
He never ever takes it off
    and wears it all the time.

He wears it through the sunny day
    and through the starry night
and bathing in the tub he does
    his laundry the same time.

This lets him save the precious water
    and conserve his time
providing him with more resources
    for his leisure life.

Some say he's quite ingenious,
    and others say he's crazy
but Emp'ror Norton works real hard
    at being very lazy.

Then after he has lathered
    and rinsed himself some more
there's still a tub of soapy suds
    to mop the kitchen floor.

The Ballad of Emperor Norton

And after everything is clean
    there is no time to rest,
he hurries out his building's door
    before he makes a mess.

In Norton's mind the place is straight
    as long as it's not shown.
His place will never look a wreck
    whenever he's not home.

Then stepping in the open air
    he swells with self-esteem,
realizing he had just invented
    the wondrous washing machine.

Then at a brisk and rapid pace
    he marches down the street
to give one last refreshing touch
    by drying in the breeze.

Emperor Norton's parade with the parrots

While strolling down the avenue
    he is surprised in that
a flock of parrots circle him
    to feather his smart cap.

Although he loves the company —
    a flashy, squawking storm,
he has some trepidations
    they'll splotch his uniform.

But after he considers this
    he solves it like a riddle,
a spot from them would be no stain,
    he'd wear it like a medal.

In fact, the spot would be an honor
    of a civic deed,
what falls onto his uniform
    won't soil the pristine street.

Then strolling down Columbus
    that intersects Broadway
the parrots swirl over his head
    just like his own parade.

Emperor Norton takes a stand against exploitation

Arriving at his daily post
    from where he guards the bay,
he looks around to see just how
    he'll brighten someone's day.

He never has to wait for long
    before his fans will gather
to have another joyful day
    of comedy and laughter.

Then from the jolly, happy crowd
    shenanigans begin
when someone with the newspaper
    shows something set in print.

Then flattening the wrinkled page
    and making a crisp fold,
the man commands the group's attention
    and hoarsely clears his throat.

"Most Noble Emp'ror Norton
    you continue to amaze
how you can manage all you do
    in your devoted days.

Taking a Stand Against Exploitation

"Each day you are out on the street
    providing public service
yet still you have enough spare time
    to publish in the journal.

"Now every morning lines will form
    to buy a single page.
The people cannot wait to read —
    The Emperor's Daily Phrase!

"Thank you for your devoted work
    by writing journalism
and sharing your enlightenment
    with daily aphorisms."

Now Norton's friends are all befuddled,
    they thought they'd known him well,
yet there are some new revelations
    nobody can foretell.

This serves to once again remind
    what everyone suspects,
all that they can expect from Norton
    is the unexpected.

Then Emp'ror Norton seems to swell
    as if he fills with pride
but Norton hopes that all his boasts
    conceal his own surprise.

The Ballad of Emperor Norton

He is reluctant to admit
    and will not dare disclose
that he is authoring a page
    he did not know he wrote.

Then raising up his calming hand
    to settle down the crowd
he uses his authority
    to figure all this out.

"I'm pleased my contributions
    that I have humbly made
are helping boost the newspaper
    so it may circulate.

"But out of curiosity
    tell us without delay
what did the paper put in print
    that I have said today?"

So once again there is a pause
    of hushed astonishment
because the Emp'ror Norton
    out did himself again.

This time they are bewildered,
    more than they'd ever known,
how could he write what he had said
    and not know what he spoke?

Taking a Stand Against Exploitation

You see the paper often used
    the Emp'ror Norton's name
but sometimes statements they would print
    are ones he had not made.

Then from the crowd one swaggers forth
    and wryly tips his hat
not to offend the lofty place
    of crown or jester cap.

"My royal heinie Emperor
    please let me get this straight,
you write your own newspaper page
    but don't know what you say?"

This was an awkward moment,
    their faces all went blank
and nothing but the squawking parrots
    filled the empty space.

But Emp'ror Norton is not fazed,
    he's comfortably at home,
these solid rock dilemmas are
    where he secures his throne.

Of all the music people play,
    and all that they may sing,
they know that Norton's clever steps
    can dance by anything.

The Ballad of Emperor Norton

His scabbard does not need a sword,
    there's flowers there today,
yet he is always quite prepared
    for any wry parley.

The crowd looks up to Norton,
    relying on his lead,
and calmly he addresses them
    to set their minds at ease.

"My loyal, faithful subjects,
    please don't become dismayed.
I hear myself talk all the time,
    I know just what I say.

"There is a reason that I ask,
    don't think this is a joke,
I want to be completely sure
    you read all that I wrote.

"Aside from my accomplishments
    of all one can report,
my greatest strength I have is from
    the strength of my support.

"And of my regal qualities
    and every single boast
my meekness and humility
    are what I pride the most.

Taking a Stand Against Exploitation

"I have the strength enough to say
    I need your help today
because with all that I have wrote
    I still have not been paid.

"I need for you to read for me
    so I can check and see
if they have printed by mistake
    egregious fallacies.

"So if you would be kind enough
    to slowly read the print,
and help me carefully inspect
    to proof the editing.

"Then finding something that offends
    like bowdlerization,
you know that I will gladly share
    what's gained in compensation."

Now no one could feel miffed with this,
    and no one could complain,
since after all the Emperor
    had said he'd share his pay.

Yet none of them considered
    and none could make report
if Norton ever had been paid
    for anything before.

The Ballad of Emperor Norton

The crowd once more turns to the man
    who holds the daily paper
and once again he clears his throat
    and reads what Norton stated.

"On this most cheerful April day,
    it is the very first,
we all must pause to contemplate
    the Emperor's wise words.

"And through his wondrous wisdom
    he generously shares,
may all our loads be lightened
    from burdens that we bear.

"And with his brilliant guidance
    from what he knows is best,
he answers questions no one asks
    with what we'd never guess.

"So on this day as any day
    believe this is no jest
attend upon our Emp'ror Norton
    and what he has professed..."

Then suddenly one interjects:
    "This must be Norton's coin!
This blustery pontification
    does not have a point!"

Taking a Stand Against Exploitation

There are some sneers and chortled snorts
    but Norton does protest,
since he has the authority
    to speak on his behest.

"Please be so kind my gentle friends
    for the formality,
the frills and trills of this prologue
    will frame my wise decree.

"Let us ignore the interruptions
    causing this delay.
Kind sir resume your heraldry
    of what I have proclaimed."

The man lifts up the newspaper
    to see where he left off
and finds the place where they had been
    before the foppish scoff.

"This newest day we've ever known
    allows us to announce
what our most Noble Emperor
    has regally pronounced.

"And then if questions still remain,
    the Emperor indeed
will gladly give more clarity
    for just a modest fee."

The Ballad of Emperor Norton

Then Emp'ror Norton nods his head
    enthusiastically,
as if confirming that he does
    wholeheartedly agree.

"Without a moment more to wait
    with stuffed formalities,
please gather up to pay attention
    and listen carefully.

"The Majestic Emp'ror Norton
    wants to relieve our sorrow
with his magnanimous decree —
    'FREE BEER FOR ALL TOMORROW!'"

With this there is a wild uproar
    and raptures of sweet bliss
as Emp'ror Norton had fulfilled
    the men's most precious wish.

But the excitement fizzles flat
    as Norton shakes his head,
apparently he disapproves
    with what they claim he said.

Then someone pleas with dour despair,
    depressed with disappointment
as if the Emperor rejects
    his spirited anointment.

Taking a Stand Against Exploitation

"Don't dare to try denying this
    or shirk away my friend
when everyone can see your statement
    clearly set in print."

Then Emp'ror Norton takes a breath
    and lets them settle down
and then he speaks to clear the air
    with wisdom fresh and sound.

"Please stop to listen faithful friends
    and do not be deceived,
this newspaper has published what
    is not my own decree.

"I never made that teasing phrase
    that's said a million times.
That promise has been made before
    but never ever binds.

"There are the passages of time,
    the wondrous moon and sun
but even for eternity
    tomorrow never comes.

"This is not something that I spoke,
    no matter what they claim.
They certainly put into print
    a phrase I didn't say.

The Ballad of Emperor Norton

"There may be complications,
　　like who is going to pay,
but the decree of Norton is —
　　FREE BEER FOR ALL TODAY!"

Emperor Norton rallies his troops

The final word that Norton said
    has saved the day again
except for just one last detail
    that stubbornly remains.

Each person in the crowd agrees
    he has a great idea,
yet no one knows for certain
    who'll offer the free beer.

If some are paid to brew and serve
    then one would have to think
that others should be paid as well
    to take a sip of drink.

And everyone in this mild crowd
    is generous indeed
and they would gladly volunteer
    to do this job for free.

As everyone is capable
    to do some sort of task
yet for this rare and special skill
    none of them have been asked.

The Ballad of Emperor Norton

And every time they've volunteered
    for every drink they take,
there's always been the stern demand
    that they're required to pay.

Then someone asks the question
    for another time —
"Of all the news that Norton's made
    he's never got a dime?"

If Norton sells the newspapers
    that people wait to buy,
he needs his rightful compensation
    for the trade he plies.

And with his gracious character
    and mirthful, merry cheer
he'd gladly take all of his pay
    in barrels of free beer.

So the Majestic Emperor
    takes hold the situation
since he's appointed it to be
    the duty of his station.

He lifts his arms to calm the crowd
    and gains all their attention,
then Norton offers his wise words
    to clear them from contention:

Emperor Norton Rallies His Troops

"Again we feel the laden weight
    each one of us must schlep
and we all know the Emperor
    must lug the greatest heft.

"And in these dire and troubling times
    of hardship and abuse,
the Emperor must lift himself
    and all his subjects too.

"The Emperor does more than rule
    the measure of his realm.
The Emperor must also guide
    and sternly hold the helm.

"So even though our seas be dry,
    as dry as our parched throats,
and lack the legal currencies
    to keep our boats afloat

"I'll steer us straight into the place —
    this paper's business office,
and there'll we'll make our just demands
    they open up their coffers.

"As Emperor I do believe
    in the economy
but we would lose all value if
    my services were free.

The Ballad of Emperor Norton

"And lacking all the pay I've earned
    how could I bear to live.
The Emperor is due tribute
    for services I give.

"With the success that I enjoy
    in ventures such as this,
I may persist to lead us all
    to joy and happiness.

"So let us march straight to this place
    where I can have my say,
for all our town's felicity
    Norton must be paid!"

Emperor Norton leads the siege upon the Fortress of Oppression

So the valiant Emp'ror Norton
 goes tilting down the street,
galumphing on his errant quest
 to claim his proper fee.

And at his side his followers
 are marching with him too
to offer their devoted aid
 to see him get his due.

But some are sure to be convinced
 that what the crowd desires
is not the joisting but the jests
 of all that will transpire.

From all their work and labor
 they do not want to fight.
The quest that they are really on
 is having a good time.

And as they stride the city blocks
 at a determined pace
soon Norton and his yeoman band
 all reach the business place.

The Ballad of Emperor Norton

The building's like a castle
    with walls up to the sky
and they believe this enterprise
    should treat it's workers right.

By using Norton's royal seat
    and celebrated fame,
this daily publication
    should give him proper pay.

They find the gated entrance.
    The moat's a busy street.
The open windows overhead
    all click with typing keys.

And stepping in the marble hall
    determined for the best,
the jolly group march straight up to
    the posted guard's oak desk.

Then with courageous confidence
    and his regality
the Emp'ror Norton and his team
    begin diplomacy.

"I greet you noble citizen
    and ask for your assistance,
there seems to be a mild offense
    requiring your attention.

The Siege of the Fortress of Oppression

"I'm sure you know just who I am,
    my name is quite renown,
I am the Royal Emperor.
    I won't be pushed around.

"Respecting this establishment
    and services performed
disseminating current news
    so people stay informed,

"there seems to be an oversight
    from columns that I wrote,
my priceless wisdom is not free —
    I'm claiming what I'm owed.

"You see a section of the paper
    printed quotes by me.
If you are printing what I say
    there is an honest fee.

"Please do not be intimidated.
    I come in here in peace.
The army in my company
    are just escorting me.

"As guard you're not the one to blame
    but don't obstruct my path.
I'm bold yet I am merciful —
    I'll spare you from my wrath.

The Ballad of Emperor Norton

"We are not looking for a brawl
    but I must have my say,
if I am selling your paper
    then I demand my pay!"

The guard is quite professional,
    respectful and polite
but has to giggle just a little
    at Norton's blusterous gripe.

"Please take a seat across the hall"
    the guard most gently says,
"so I can call the editor
    to answer your request."

Now Emp'ror Norton is quite pleased
    the guard is serious,
yet not completely confident
    with his inept judgement.

So Emp'ror Norton once again
    is troubled with some doubt
and offers more of his insight
    to point the issue out.

"Feel free to call the editor.
    I know just how to spell.
But don't you think it best to call
    accounting personnel?"

The Siege of the Fortress of Oppression

So after stating his demands
    then Norton and his team
all walk across the narrow hall
    and calmly take their seats.

They mustered all their forces
    to make a fearsome siege
but of their staged theatrics
    they hardly made a scene.

They came in search for glory
    but are a touch confused —
how is it their ferocious charge
    turned to the waiting room?

The Fearsome Battle Ensues!

They take their seats politely
    to rest their weary plight
but something quite peculiar
    catches Norton's eye.

When all his subjects take a rest,
    the Emp'ror stays alert,
a leader's always on the guard,
    that's how respect is earned.

Although the others do not see,
    their focus must have slipped,
the keen sight of the Emperor
    sees something that's amiss.

Ten paces down the marble hall
    a man in uniform
is standing stout and purposeful
    inside an open door.

What others may not notice,
    gives Norton a clear clue,
it's odd to see a soldier guard
    a tiny, empty room.

The Fearsome Battle

If the paper can afford to pay
    for this boondoggling,
for certain they can satisfy
    Norton's modest fee.

He has responsibilities
    heavy and abundant,
so many people's happiness
    rely upon his judgement.

His reputation is well known
    and honored through the town.
His status is outstanding
    even when he's sitting down.

Deciding to investigate
    the doubtful situation,
he strolls the length of the great hall
    to gain more information.

Then pacing down a straightened path,
    as narrow as a plank,
he speaks with an authority
    assured with his high rank.

"Please pardon me if I disturb
    your focused concentration,
but I am very curious
    about your occupation.

The Ballad of Emperor Norton

"Your uniform is fine and clean,
    your creases razor sharp,
and for the humble rank you hold
    you surely play your part."

Then Norton notes the soldier has
    no medals on his chest,
believing he's a new recruit
    with no experience.

Then Emp'ror Norton cannot help
    to swell with his own pride —
his chest is covered with awards
    of stains from beer and wine.

Assured that he can keep his tack
    he ventures out to ask,
since he is at the newspaper
    he wants the cold, hard facts.

"Attention soldier, just a word,
    I've something I must say,
you're diligent and dutiful
    but puzzle me today.

"For honor and for duty,
    I order you to answer,
why you're assignment is to guard
    a tiny, empty chamber?"

The Fearsome Battle

The guard is certainly prepared
    and knows his designation,
responding to the Emperor
    without a hesitation.

"I'm grateful you appreciate
    my faithful dedication
attending the new elevator
    for its operation."

This said, the gentleman returns
    to his assigned profession.
He seems assured he had answered
    Norton's plucky question.

But Norton is not satisfied
    with what the man had said.
He does not feel the man is brusque,
    but just a smudged bit vague.

So Norton asks another time
    to get at all the truth
and find exactly what it is
    he is assigned to do.

"I much admire your stoical
    laconic reticence
but I am puzzled by your job
    so thus I must persist.

The Ballad of Emperor Norton

"You're dutifully devoted
    but I'm a bit confused
just why you are assigned to guard
    this tiny, empty room."

The gentleman first nods his head
    in a respectful way
but is unsure about what more
    remains to be explained.

Then he suspects that Norton's deaf,
    at least in that one ear,
and leans off to the other side
    to trumpet loud and clear.

"This is a new invention,
    an Acme Elevator,
and I have been assigned to be
    official operator.

"It was installed just months ago
    at a substantial cost,
the very first one to exist
    on California's coast.

"I hope my explanation
    answers all your questions.
Please pardon me so that I may
    return to my profession."

The Fearsome Battle

The Emperor is courteous
    and gives the man a break.
His job's explained by what he does
    that's all he needs to say.

For Emp'ror Norton to persist
    in questioning the man,
then Norton would have to admit
    he does not understand.

Yet far from being satisfied
    Norton won't let go.
He's sure the man's not telling all
    of what he seems to know.

In fact the guard's elusive language
    makes him more suspect.
There must be something going on
    he's trying to protect.

Norton's known some aggravators
    and some instigators
but never once has he heard of
    an Acme Elevator.

So he decides to step aside
    in due consideration
and make adjustments to find out
    with quiet observation.

The Ballad of Emperor Norton

He saunters over to the side
    and tries to be discrete
but as the town's celebrity
    this is no simple feat.

To stand atop the pinnacle
    requires a careful balance
yet doing the impossible
    is one of his best talents.

So, when he's out in public view
    and needs a sly disguise,
he simply whistles obscure tunes
    no one can recognize.

Then paying off his patience,
    he gains his bounty's boon
and sees two people walking past
    then step into the room.

They're greeted by the guard who turns
    to welcome them aboard
and Norton acts distracted till
    they've closed and latched the door.

When they're inside a frightful sound
    makes Norton flinch and start,
a fierce machine that clacks and clangs
    cold steel without a heart.

The Fearsome Battle

And even though he'd never seen
    those people who walked by
it is his duty to make sure
    those people are alright.

And then with all the frightful noise
    it raises an alarm,
and Norton cringes with concern
    if they are safe from harm.

In fact with all the banging noise —
    a clashing, groaning strain,
there is concern that the machine
    may also be in pain.

Then suffering for minutes
    Norton almost cries
because with what he witnesses
    he can't believe his eyes.

Two people had walked in the room,
    of this he has no doubt,
but when the door opens again
    just one man walks back out!

The Emperor is terror struck
    but knows he must report this
but wisely he goes to his friends
    to gather reinforcements.

The Ballad of Emperor Norton

Then Norton runs back to his friends
    as if about to burst
and they are all astonished that
    he's at a loss of words.

It's not as if the Emperor
    has nothing left to say,
he doesn't want to blow his cover
    and give himself away.

He huffs and puffs excitedly
    and waves his men with him
and they all rush along to see
    what Norton had witnessed.

Then standing off onto the side
    a disconcerted crowd,
they pause to wait so they can see
    what this is all about.

Then Norton gives a subtle sign,
    as people walk on by,
the group of men try not to stare
    as if preoccupied.

They watch the people greet the guard
    and step into the room
where Emp'ror Norton is convinced
    the group will meet their doom.

The Fearsome Battle

The heavy metal door slides shut
    and rumbling begins,
a fearful working of machines,
    a clashing, gnashing din.

Then after a few minutes wait
    the door opens again
but all alone the soldier stands
    and wears a happy grin.

The guard is just acknowledging
    admirers of his trade
but Norton sees a twisted smirk
    that makes a wicked face.

Perhaps it's just a magic trick
    of that they are not clear
but people had walked in that room
    and then they disappeared!

Continuing to wait and watch
    none of them can believe
why anyone would want to build
    this scandalous machine.

They watch as the machine transforms
    a man into a woman
and then again thereafter
    a woman to a man.

The Ballad of Emperor Norton

They find themselves completely vexed
    at this monstrous machine
transforming different people
    to what they hadn't been.

In dread and fear the men all stand
    in their perplexity
then all together turn to Norton
    in hope for clarity.

Before the Emperor can speak
    and share his light for all,
they hear a sudden summoning
    announcement down the hall.

"Most Noble Emp'ror Norton
    as with no more ado,
one of our friendly editors
    is here to speak with you.

"This is the first that he has heard
    of the complaint you raised.
You said somehow the newspaper
    is owing you some pay.

"The editor kindly agrees
    to give some of his time
so that we may address this case
    and get our books in line."

The Fearsome Battle

Then stepping with his right foot first
    assured of his firm place,
the editor walks up to Norton
    to meet him face to face.

Then straightening his spectacles
    to square them on his nose,
the editor politely states
    all that of what he knows:

"Most Noble Norton I've been told
    you issued a complaint
that our respectful newspaper
    has been withholding pay.

"Although I'm not completely sure
    what all this may pertain.
I will be happy to resolve
    your grievances and pain.

"If you don't mind to be so kind
    and walk a while with me
and join me in my office
    and talk till we agree."

The Emperor is pleased to be
    addressed respectfully
and then begins to ply some more
    to further press his plea.

The Ballad of Emperor Norton

"I'm grateful Mr. Editor
    you're offering your time
to listen to my grievances
    of what I've been denied.

"I'm absolutely confident
    in finding a solution
and from your paper I expect
    an ample restitution."

The Emperor is plumply pleased
    so far as he can see
and finds they're off to a good start
    on terms agreeably.

The editor leads cordially
    while walking down the hall
then something catches Norton's eye
    that makes a sudden qualm.

Then Norton wisely stalls them all
    and raises an alarm
while looking toward the tiny room
    manned by the grinning guard.

"I'm grateful that you have agreed
    to kindly hear my plea
but I'm a little bit concerned
    exactly where you lead."

The Fearsome Battle

The editor is very clear
    and does not mince his words,
he goes straight to the point without
    a parenthetic turn.

"We're going to my office now
    to sit and talk at ease
and there we'll comfortably converse
    until we can agree.

"I'm sure you'll find that I can be
    a fair negotiator,
my office is on the top floor,
    let's take the elevator."

When Norton hears these fearful words
    he almost hits the floor
then looks up at the saucy guard
    who's grinning at the door.

Then Norton turns back to his friends,
    they are as scared as he,
and he can clearly recognize
    it's time for them to leave.

So Emp'ror Norton takes command
    and with his stalwart lead,
they quickly pivot in the hall
    and run at breakneck speed.

The Ballad of Emperor Norton

The editor stands baffled,
    the guard, he keeps his smile,
and Norton and the party
    run for miles and miles.

Part III

The Trial of Emperor Norton

Emperor Norton
plays the Market

To start another gorgeous day
    before the city stirs
the faithful Emp'ror Norton
    is singing with the birds.

He never shirks his civic duties,
    each day throughout the year,
to keep each person's spirits up
    with laughter and good cheer.

But following along to hear
    of all his jocund tales
there are some questions that arise
    of what his life entails.

The Emperor is generous
    with all the joy he gives
but people often ask just how
    he can afford to live.

Most people have to work each day
    to pay for their free time
but how can he support himself
    by having a good time?

Emperor Norton Plays the Market

It's easy to be critical
    of daily obligations
but managing his louche lifestyle
    is Norton's occupation.

His life is always full of fun
    with laughter and good thrills
but how can he produce the funds
    to pay all of his bills?

Some people think the Emperor
    is always drinking beer
but people do not recognize
    he is a financier.

Some may believe this is a stretch,
    another fantasy,
but Norton plays a crucial role
    in the economy.

He has a local printing shop
    make up his special bonds
he circulates out in the street
    near home and far beyond.

They're dignified with his image
    — the seated Emperor,
and are endorsed officially
    with his bold signature.

The Ballad of Emperor Norton

The filigree design he made
    is his own masterpiece.
He even keeps one in a frame
    that people pay to see.

And given Norton's honesty
    and credibility
no one could have a doubt about
    the bond's validity.

The bonds return a stellar yield
    with steep appreciation
for people in possession of
    a good imagination.

For no more than a dollar bill
    and just a little wait
the bond will give five dollars back
    on a specific date.

But Norton thinks they're all unique
    exquisite artistry,
why would someone exchange them for
    a common currency?

They may not be the gold standard
    and can't be used as cash,
however they are always worth
    a good and hearty laugh.

Emperor Norton Plays the Market

But Norton is not so naive
    that he would not suspect
that someone would return to him
    expecting to collect.

And when that time comes passing by
    when all the bonds mature,
the unsold bonds he keeps himself
    will make him rich for sure.

Yet as we all have seen before
    the Emp'ror has his tests
and of the wonders of his life
    some always will protest.

A man confronts the Emperor
    who looks to be important.
He is a man the day before
    had bought a bond from Norton.

With all of the familiar crowd
    now gathered into place
the gentleman who has returned
    begins to vent his rage.

He says he visited the bank
    to check the bond he bought,
the teller at the bank told him
    the bond is a true fraud.

The Ballad of Emperor Norton

So as the people gather round
 to hear the man's complaint,
they hold an open public court
 to settle what is claimed.

If anyone still has a doubt
 remaining in denial
this is the legendary tale
 of Emp'ror Norton's trial.

An Unhappy Customer takes Emperor Norton to Court

Now with the crowd all gathered round
    they have all that they need
to call to order for a trial
    and legally proceed.

At least that is what some would hope
    of lawful situations
but Norton's life always involves
    unruly complications.

Yet Norton's life is not about
    heartbreaking tragedies
when all he does turns out to be
    delightful comedies.

The plaintiff sternly takes his stand
    with heated accusations
and Emp'ror Norton is perplexed
    with the insinuations.

Both men believe they have a case
    the other is to blame
and even with their differences
    they both make this same claim.

The Ballad of Emperor Norton

They both need to be heard in court
    to see who's on the right
and then they'll judge who is at fault
    until appeals are filed.

Of course this must be carried out
    in civic minded ways.
They can't just bicker on forever,
    a court must be arranged.

The bailiff is a traffic guard
    to guide how this proceeds.
The press is by the paper boy
    who sells news on the street.

And for the most judicious mind
    with her impartial powers
the judge appointed to the court
    — the lady who sells flowers.

Now these appointments can be made
    direct and easily
but the selection of the jury
    is far more challenging.

A call is made for citizens
    throughout the social circuit
so thoughtful people can be chose
    to make the final verdict.

Emperor Norton in Court

There is the word of public duty
    by which they're asked to serve
but at the start of the selection
    a single voice is heard:

"When I am asked to serve the public
    I'm first before I'm last.
Now that we are all summoned here
    there's something I must ask.

"A jury of one's civic peers
    is a necessity,
how else can justice ever be
    with fair equality?

"When we consider Emp'ror Norton
    there's something that's unclear —
how can a jury be arranged
    for someone without peers?"

This stirs some talk within the crowd
    of which some will concede
without a jury of his peers
    how can the trial proceed?

The judge is very scrupulous
    with honor and esteem
then weighs the matter in her mind
    with equanimity:

The Ballad of Emperor Norton

"The court acknowledges the statement
    that is sincerely made
but there is one assured response
    of which I will make plain.

"There are peculiarities
    for Norton's qualities
and certainly we all agree
    that he is most unique.

"But something no one can deny
    as we have all been taught
no person in the whole wide world
    can be above the law.

"And even though the Emperor
    has eccentricities,
his case must be considered with
    impartiality.

"Although he is the Emperor
    and holds a noble seat,
he only holds the power that
    the people will concede.

"And even with his uniform,
    awards and epaulets,
he is a person like us all
    we mutually respect.

Emperor Norton in Court

"Although his rank may be up high
    in our society,
what we can all relate with him
    is his humanity.

"And even if we look to him
    for leadership of sorts,
the high position that he holds
    is from all our support.

"A pageant needs an audience
    as hotdogs need a bun,
and any joke that is not heard
    is never any fun.

"And though we may depend on him
    for his regal report,
don't ever doubt the Emperor
    needs us a whole lot more.

"Composing all society
    in its entirety
as judge I will make my decree —
    you're all on the jury."

And with the judge's wise guidance
    and with the book of law,
the complications are worked out,
    the issue is resolved.

The Ballad of Emperor Norton

Now that there's order to the court
    they open up the case
and everyone anticipates
    there'll be another fray.

The plaintiff walks up to the bench
    from his offended place
pontificating to the court
    to make his sore complaint.

"On yesterday while walking down
    the street in the fresh air
I bumped into this ribald guy
    you call the Emperor.

"I thought he was a gentleman,
    at first I was impressed,
although I know I was deceived
    right now in retrospect.

"He has his eccentricities
    but that is not a crime,
I too have unique qualities
    especially all mine.

"But then he started to show me
    his civic service bond.
He seemed sincere and genial
    and not a cutthroat con.

Emperor Norton in Court

"The bond had a fantastic yield,
    I'd never seen one better,
and I believe myself to be
    a very shrewd investor.

"I am a very modest man.
    I don't have funds to burn.
The bond cost just one dollar bill
    then earned five in return

"and since I am from out of town
    and living in the rough
with this assistance offered me,
    how could I pass that up?

"But when I went into a bank
    to show the bond I bought,
the teller told me that the bond
    is certainly a fraud!"

And when the man had reached the end,
    he had begun to shout,
and his uproar of scandal sent
    a shudder through the crowd.

But Norton listened carefully
    and could not be disturbed.
The piping tantrum of the man
    was just a bunch of words.

The Ballad of Emperor Norton

And without doubt the Emperor
    had heard all this before.
However much the man might say,
    then Norton could say more.

Then with his calm demeanor
    the Emperor replies,
he can pile on enough manure
    where mountains may all hide.

"You claim you are an investor
    in our economy,
I would expect you to possess
    a sharp sagacity.

"I do not know who you consult
    or pay your broker fees
or what position that they hold
    or their authority.

"But commerce is an interaction,
    a regular exchange,
and through a building circulation
    value appreciates.

"We manufacture what we need
    and try to find a bargain
for fabrication of ideas
    we put out in the market.

Emperor Norton in Court

"We trade the tools and the produce
    and such commodities
and do our best to satisfy
    whatever are our needs.

"I have no aim to disappoint
    or cause someone to grieve.
My aim is always happiness.
    I always try to please.

"And of the joy I bring to all
    you certainly can find
abundantly providing through
    my service to mankind.

"I'm always happy to engage
    in cordial exchange
to currently invest the time
    and tenderly explain.

"Your dollar is a simple page
    of paper printed plain.
The bond that you had purchased here
    was printed the same way.

"How can you claim that one has wealth,
    the other without worth,
that one is certain for the better,
    the other for the worse?

The Ballad of Emperor Norton

"One may be held as legal tender
    but where had it been mined?
It doesn't even have a trace
    of silver in a dime.

"And with the bond I offer you
    more than a simple token,
I'm giving courtly friendliness
    and isn't friendship golden?

"My bond is quite a rarity,
    unique in our own time,
as it is overflowing with
    the bounty of my mind.

"And of these people gathered here,
    a cheery population,
it is accepted welcomingly —
    a true denomination.

"Just show this bond to anyone
    collected in this trial,
it promptly will be reimbursed
    with warm and hearty smiles.

"Through the devotions of your life —
    your labor and unrest,
you ultimately want to gain
    a wealth of happiness.

Emperor Norton in Court

"Of all that you have labored for
    and hope to find in life,
my treasury's all mirth and joy
    and riches of delight!"

The plaintiff has some dizziness
    and wobbles on his feet
and tries to follow all the loops
    of Norton's specious speech.

He then decides a new approach
    for yet another round
and focus on a single point
    to pin the Emp'ror down.

"I will acknowledge your response
    although I still contend
your fabricating industry
    does not make any sense.

"There is one thing you can't deny
    across this entire land
your regal seat as Emperor
    is certainly a sham!

"I am not sure where you may live
    or think that you exist,
the country where you are right now
    is a strong Republic.

The Ballad of Emperor Norton

"The only place where you may rule
    and claim as your Empire
is the ridiculous frontier
    in your deluded mind."

At all these childish accusations
    Norton is not shocked.
He's heard them all a thousand times
    they are of common stock.

However in the legalese
    it's called an argument,
the Emp'ror gives his calm response
    with his cool countenance.

And with proud Norton's wise, thick beard
    he wouldn't stoop to bicker,
and gives reply without a strain
    of any of his whiskers.

"My ruling seat as Emperor
    has been besieged before
and I don't have a single doubt
    it will be challenged more.

"But everyone who's gathered here
    will holler to confirm —
despite the tests and trials I've had
    my office is held firm.

Emperor Norton in Court

"Don't quibble about government
    — that is not any fun.
That's why we made a government
    of representation.

"The Capitol is in D.C.
    where politicians run.
We choose officials by our vote
    to fight in Washington.

"But there is one important point
    that I will help you see,
all the protections put in place
    for local sovereignty!

"The population can't be ruled
    by pompous overlords,
that was the reason that we had
    our Revolution for.

"We have our civil freedoms here
    of this I am convinced,
don't mind me while I exercise
    my independence

"respecting others as myself
    in each and every way,
promoting life and liberty
    and happiness all day!

The Ballad of Emperor Norton

"And of the people all around
    most everyone agrees
I am the local Emperor
    out on the friendly streets.

"And what I govern as my realm
    and where I do reside
is the one place I can control —
    it is my state of mind.

"And of this state consisting of
    my mind's capacity,
its vast expanse extends throughout
    all that I can believe!"

The plaintiff listens carefully
    to Norton's explanations
not certain what to think about
    all these confabulations.

Still he decides he will resume
    and faithfully persist
to make his claim and grievances
    in his stern argument.

"The stubborn question in this case
    is not your state of mind
or any other quality
    of some absurd design.

Emperor Norton in Court

"By marketing and selling bonds
    you're bound by a contract
and civil law requires that you
    must pay the money back!

"My question now is this
    and here I must be terse
where is the money you owe me
    inside your empty purse?"

With this the sovereign Emperor
    gallantly nods his head
and offers a tranquil response
    to what the man had said.

"Your slander and your calumny
    is totally undue.
I have a dollar in my purse.
    Your statement is untrue."

But then the man responds again
    enflamed in an outrage,
"That dollar you have in your purse
    I gave you yesterday!"

The judge can see the court has turned
    into a tangled fray.
She intercedes to extricate
    and straighten out the way.

The Ballad of Emperor Norton

She feels the need to interject
    to call the court to order
and firmly asks a question for
    the Noble Emp'ror Norton.

"Please tell us Mr. Emperor
    and honestly inform,
the bonds you sell out on the street —
    what are the funds used for?"

Then Norton steps out firm and proud
    and answers graciously,
there is no gimmick or snide tone
    to slur his formal speech.

"The bonds are for the public service
    addressing desperate need
that I'm devoting all my time
    to make sure it's appeased.

"I tirelessly will preach and plea
    to sell these bonds each day
to raise the funds so we may build
    a bridge across the bay."

When Emp'ror Norton has said this
    the people are all stunned
because he actually sounds as if
    he isn't making fun.

Emperor Norton in Court

The people pause to look around
    as to confirm as one
if they had heard what Norton said
    or had they come undone.

Then suddenly there is a roar
    that shakes like an earthquake
as everyone all laughs about
    what they heard Norton say.

They hop around hilarity
    while slapping on their thighs,
a few are even tipping over
    while aching at their sides.

And Norton wonders to himself
    is he delirious?
He seems to be more funny when
    he's being serious.

Then after the last giggled snick
    and everyone is calm
the plaintiff raises up his voice
    to state another qualm.

"You see how he's evading now
    to shirk away his fee!
He wants to sway the court so he
    can plead insanity."

The Ballad of Emperor Norton

Then Emp'ror Norton once again
    addresses what's at hand,
devoted in his holy boots
    to firmly take his stand.

"Each week I take the ferry boat
    to go across the bay
and I know there has got to be
    a more convenient way.

"If we could build a bridge to span
    the breadth across the bay
that'd simplify all of our lives
    in every single way.

"Then crossing over the broad bay
    wouldn't be a bother,
all that we'd ever have to do
    is walk over the water."

When they had heard what Norton said
    the people stood in awe
while squinting to envision what
    the Emp'ror clearly saw.

Then once again the sour plaintiff
    is in for one more round
and tries to make a jab and hook
    assured the Emperor's down.

Emperor Norton in Court

"This definitely is absurd.
    What fool would ever buy it?
What's next? Will he propose to build
    a bridge out to Hawaii!

"I'm sure you all are now convinced
    he's crazy as a loon.
I bet he even tries to say
    we'll make it to the moon."

To quiet all the mockery
    the judge brings court to order
to try and find a remedy
    for this confused disorder.

"The court's defense must keep in mind
    our engineering means
and carefully consider this
    a bit more reasonably.

"The engineers design a bridge
    to span a deep ravine.
There are a number of all these
    that each of us have seen.

"Yet as for what you have proposed
    the court will make a note,
still we believe the bay and sea
    are best traversed by boat.

The Ballad of Emperor Norton

"What you propose cannot be done,
    it's never been conceived.
The only way it could exist
    is in somebody's dreams."

Respectfully the Emp'ror says
    to verify his statement
and his firm place that stands within
    his wild imagination.

"But don't you see if it exists
    inside somebody's dream,
then it already has become
    part of reality.

"What we can build within our minds
    both singular and plural,
we can develop and expand
    to share with the whole world.

"They can't deny something exists
    that is already done.
To simply say things don't add up
    cannot deny the sum.

"They can't say it's impossible
    and say that it will fail
and give the reason just because
    they can't do it themselves.

Emperor Norton in Court

"Let them deny the possible
    and for themselves refuse it.
That certainly will never mean
    another cannot do it!"

Though Emp'ror Norton has been known
    to be impractical,
he has astutely made a point
    that's irrefutable.

While everyone has paused in thought
    the judge makes a provision
to steer the court so it proceeds
    in reaching a decision.

"The court's progress has somehow stalled
    from making a report
and once again I'll ask the plaintiff
    to clarify some more —

"You have complained the bond's a fraud
    so what you have implied —
you are demanding a payment
    that Norton has denied.

"There's one important detail
    that no one here has heard,
exactly what's the time and date
    when Norton's bond matures."

The Ballad of Emperor Norton

The plaintiff digs his pockets out
    and shows upon his palm
the bond that he had angrily
    crumpled in a ball.

Then flattening the wadded note
    he reads out carefully
all of the details of the terms
    that they had both agreed.

"The reimbursement of this bond
    for interest and arrears
can be requested at a time
    and Eighteen Eighty is the year."

When this is said they all are hushed
    and look up to the judge.
A calendar is all they need
    to clear all of this up.

"The plaintiff needs to understand
    and let me make it clear
our situation and the time
    and number of the year.

"It is still Eighteen Seventy Nine,
    please look at the agreement.
You can't demand your payment
    before the term's fulfillment."

Emperor Norton in Court

Then suddenly they all erupt
and shout ecstatically
because the Emp'ror Norton
is once again set free.

Epilogue —
Emperor Norton's Everlasting Day

In the year of Eighteen Eighty
    the Emp'ror is concerned
if people would begin to ask
    about the bonds he served.

He sold the bonds out on the streets,
    each one had been consigned,
and now the date they are mature
    had finally arrived.

There is a minor complication
    to promissory notes —
how could the Emp'ror ever pay
    when he is always broke?

Still Emp'ror Norton would not cower,
    he has to make his rounds,
the city would not be the same
    if he could not be found.

So, if the people make complaints
    then he would just remind them,
the bonds were made so beautifully
    they'll be collector's items.

Epilogue

The bonds will be preserved archives
    of ingenuity,
a cultural commodity
    of priceless novelty.

And so he steps out in the street
    where he is daily seen
to gather all around again
    his merry company.

But strolling down the avenue
    the Emp'ror is surprised,
nobody seems to notice
    as he is walking by.

He is the town's celebrity
    and every single day
the people would inquire about
    the Emp'ror's Golden Gate.

This day is oddly different
    and he is quite surprised
because the people that he sees
    are passing him right by.

Then standing at his normal spot
    his friends are not around.
It's like he had woke up this day
    in some uncertain town.

The Ballad of Emperor Norton

And on the sidewalk where he stands
    he's almost brought to tears
because the people pass him by
    as if he isn't there.

And then he spots to his relief
    someone he always sees —
the kid who sells the daily news
    along the busy street.

And walking toward the Emperor's
    enthusiastic wave
the kid just keeps on walking by
    without a word to say.

Then Norton watches as the kid
    employs his earnest trade
as he announces the headline
    that's printed on the page.

"Come get your daily paper
    and sadly you will read
last night the Emp'ror Norton died
    at peace in his soft sleep!"

Now Emp'ror Norton is surprised
    to hear the sad headline —
why didn't people let him know
    he died in bed last night?

Epilogue

But then to his astonishment
    a crowd along the street
is passing by and then extends
    beyond where he can see.

He doesn't know what it's about,
    it is no holiday.
It is too calm for a protest,
    too sad for a parade.

And then he sees a somber group
    who push a bier with them
but who he sees that's laid to rest —
    a man who looks like him!

So he decides that he will see
    just what is going on,
it seems a dignitary died
    for dirges played this long.

He thinks it odd the stores are closed.
    No one is seen around.
It seems that everyone in town
    has joined the mourning crowd.

They shuffle in the cemetery
    without a word to say
and stand together somberly
    around the empty grave.

The Ballad of Emperor Norton

The minister devoutly stands
 to give consoling words
and everyone stands listening
 to what they sadly heard:

"Our kind and gentle Emperor
 was cherished by us all
and it is always heartbreaking
 to see a great man fall.

"He lived a very humble life
 through dearth and modest means,
but offered an abundant wealth
 of personality.

"He dedicated his whole life
 through generosity
to offer all the joy he had
 so we'd live happily.

"Now we return with our respect
 to always know the better,
the mirth and warmth of this kind man
 will stay with us forever."

With these commemorating words
 they file throughout the day
and set at least a field of flowers
 into his open grave.

Epilogue

But Emp'ror Norton would not go
    and cries throughout the tears:
"That is not me inside the grave.
    I'm standing with you here!"

He jumps and shouts and waves his arms
    yet no one sees him though,
and they all slowly walk away
    and leave him all alone.

Then Norton looks into the grave
    when everyone has left,
accepting the reality —
    "It's no fun being dead."

Then suddenly he is surprised
    by brilliant bursts of light
and then an angel seems to float
    before his widened eyes.

Then with a humble disposition
    and words direct and plain,
the Emp'ror Norton simply asks,
    "Did I live life in vain?"

Then with a voice perfectly clear
    with calm tranquility
the angel offers a reply
    to Norton's inquiry:

The Ballad of Emperor Norton

"Joshua Norton don't despair
    for the course of your life,
every person must endure
    the trials of their own plight.

"You had such meager means
    and were beset with stress,
yet always you were offering
    boundless happiness.

"There is no shameful vanity
    for which to feel regret
to be one of the gracious ones
    who give more than they get.

"And now you may lift up your arms
    and drop your heavy stones.
Now come and fly away with me.
    I've come to take you home."

Then rising up into the sky,
    they fly directly west
and soar over the vast ocean
    for a glorious sunset.

THE END

photo © Bob Kidd
bobkiddphotography.com

Garrett Buhl Robinson is a poet living in New York City. Aside from the stories about Emperor Norton's carousing revelry, Mr. Robinson is enjoying his happiest and most productive years of his life completely sober.

If you enjoyed this ballad, you can order more books by Garrett Buhl Robinson from your favorite bookstore or request them at your local library.

More books by Garrett Buhl Robinson

<u>Poetry</u>
Pilgrims
Whispering Emily
Little Pieces of Poetry
City of Poems
The Nobody
Always Here Always Odd
Beauty beyond Reason
Martha, a poem

<u>Fiction</u>
Zoë
Nunatak

Poet in the Park
In Humanity I see Grace, Beauty and Dignity.
PoetinthePark.com

www.ingramcontent.com/pod-product-compliance
Lightning Source LLC
Chambersburg PA
CBHW060404080526
44583CB00012B/465